The Story of Flight

FLYING FOR FUN

Crabtree Publishing Company
www.crabtreebooks.com

PMB 16A, 350 Fifth Avenue,
Suite 3308
New York, NY 10118

612 Welland Avenue
St. Catharines, Ontario
L2M 5V6

Published in 2004 by
Crabtree Publishing Company

Coordinating editor: Ellen Rodger
Project editors: Sean Charlebois, Carrie Gleason
Production coordinator: Rose Gowsell

Created and Produced by
David West Children's Books

Project Development, Design, and Concept
David West Children's Books:
Designer: Gary Jeffrey
Editor: Gail Bushnell
Illustrators: Terry Pastor, Martyn Patrick, Gary Slater &
Steve Weston (Specs Art), Pete Roberts (Allied Artists),
Alain Salesse (Contact Jupiter), James Field (SGA), Alex
Pang.
Picture Research: Carlotta Cooper

Photo Credits:
Abbreviations: t-top, m-middle, b-bottom, r-right,
l-left, c-center.

Front cover & pages 4, 5, 8, 9, 10, 11, 13b, 15, 16,
17, 18t, 22t & b, 24b, 26b, 28, 29 - Steen Media. 7t
& b - Rex Features. 13t, 14, 26t - The Flight
Collection. 21, 24t - The Culture Archive. 23 - Paul
Glenshaw, Cognitive Applications Inc., USA. 25 -
ME 262 Project.

06 05 04 03
10 9 8 7 6 5 4 3 2 1

Library of Congress Cataloging-in-Publication Data
Hansen, Ole Steen.
   Flying for Fun / written by Ole Steen Hansen.
      p. cm. -- (The story of flight)
Includes index.
Contents: Ballooning -- The birth of gliding -- Modern gliding --
Learning to fly -- Homebuilds -- Modern light aircraft -- Ultralights --
Air racing -- Flying vintage aircraft -- Warbirds -- Aerobatics -- Model
aircraft.
   ISBN 0-7787-1211-7 (RLB : alk. paper) -- ISBN 0-7787-1227-3 (PB
: alk. paper)
   1. Aeronautics--Juvenile literature. 2. Aeronautical sports--Juvenile
literature. [1. Aeronautics. 2. Aeronautical sports.] I. Title. II. Series.
   TL547.H153 2003
   629.13--dc22
                                                        2003016197

The Story of Flight

FLYING FOR FUN

Ole Steen Hansen

 Crabtree Publishing Company
www.crabtreebooks.com

CONTENTS

CESSNA 172
A short flight for fun over a coast in a Cessna 172.

INTRODUCTION

Flying is a useful means of transportation. Flying is necessary for business, for a country's military defense, and for going on vacation. Flying is also fun, especially flying light planes, gliders, balloons, micro lights, warbirds, or aircraft you have built yourself!

SMALL IS BEAUTIFUL!
It looks like a toy, but it is actually a Hummel homebuilt, a tiny single seat all metal aircraft. It cruises at almost 100 mph (161 km/h).

BLASTING INTO THE SKY
Airshows are a chance to see aircraft perform aerobatics. Most shows feature old planes and new ones doing loops, rolls, and stall turns.

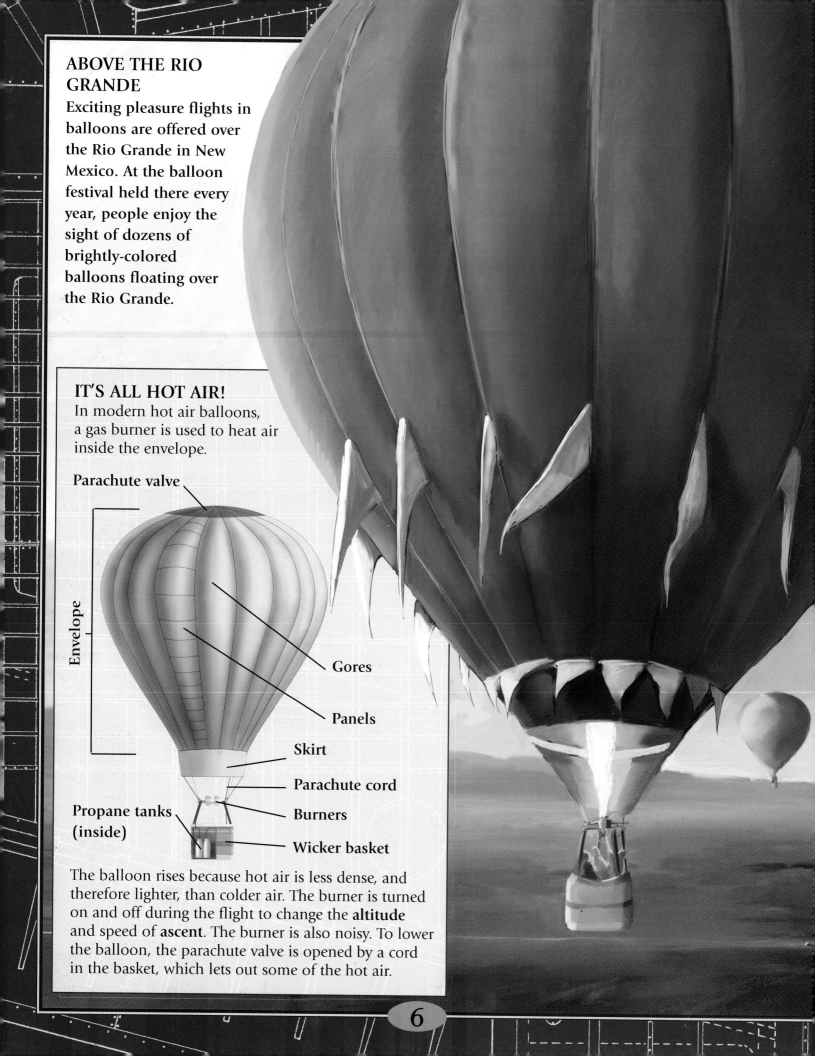

ABOVE THE RIO GRANDE

Exciting pleasure flights in balloons are offered over the Rio Grande in New Mexico. At the balloon festival held there every year, people enjoy the sight of dozens of brightly-colored balloons floating over the Rio Grande.

IT'S ALL HOT AIR!

In modern hot air balloons, a gas burner is used to heat air inside the envelope.

Parachute valve

Envelope

Gores

Panels

Skirt

Parachute cord

Propane tanks (inside)

Burners

Wicker basket

The balloon rises because hot air is less dense, and therefore lighter, than colder air. The burner is turned on and off during the flight to change the **altitude** and speed of **ascent**. The burner is also noisy. To lower the balloon, the parachute valve is opened by a cord in the basket, which lets out some of the hot air.

BALLOONING

The first manned balloon flight took place in November 1783, when two men flew a hot air balloon over Paris, France. Today, hot air balloons are still popular among people who want to feel like they are floating above ground.

In the early days of ballooning, hydrogen-filled balloons were common. Hydrogen has more lifting power than hot air and was used by the big **airships** before **World War II**. Hydrogen is a **flammable** gas, so a leaky balloon was dangerous. Helium is another gas used in balloons.

Helium does not burn, but it has less lifting power and is expensive to use. Balloons filled with hot air are some of the most practical flying machines. When you are finished flying, you just let the air out, roll up the balloon, and celebrate your happy landing!

SOLO BALLOONS

Is this a picture of a parachute that goes up instead of down? No, this is flying by hanging in a harness under a balloon. Solo balloons are flown without a basket by one person in a chair attached to the balloon.

Around the World

For years, people had been attempting to sail around the world in balloons. On March 20, 1999, Bertrand Piccard of Switzerland, and pilot Brian Jones of Britain landed after flying their hot air balloon around the world. It took them 19 days, 21 hours, and 55 minutes to fly around the Earth.

THE BIRTH OF GLIDING

The Wright brothers experimented with gliders before flying the world's first powered aircraft in 1903. It was only after World War I that gliding became a sport.

OLYMPIA GLIDER

The Olympia was designed as a standard glider for the Olympics. Gliding never became an Olympic sport, but the Olympia was and still is an excellent glider. It was built in several countries.

THE VAMPYR

In 1922 the German Vampyr became the first glider to fly for over an hour. It was a very sleek and advanced design for its day. Most powered aircraft in 1922 were bulky biplanes with struts and bracing wires.

For years after World War I, the Germans were not allowed to build powered aircraft. Instead, they built gliders, and discovered how fun and challenging it was to fly them. A glider has no engine and must always **descend** to maintain speed, similar to the way a bicycle goes downhill without being pedaled. Gliders stay in the air by riding on air currents. To climb, the glider has to find a current of air that is rising faster than the glider is descending.

GETTING LIFT

In the 1920s, gliders stayed up using the winds that are forced up over hills, cliffs, and high dunes by the sea. Years later, glider pilots discovered that they could rise with thermals, or columns of hot rising air. Today, using thermals is the most common way for gliders to climb.

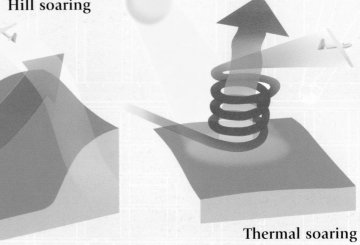

Hill soaring

Thermal soaring

Flights of more than 40 hours were eventually made in the fast-moving air that is pushed over high dunes by the sea. In the open cockpit, glider pilots just flew back and forth in the wind. Germany became the center of gliding, but pilots from other countries soon took up the new sport. Plans were made to make gliding an Olympic sport, but World War II stopped that project. Gliding competitions are still held today in some countries.

Single Seat Training

A sailplane is a very light glider built especially for soaring. Sailplanes and soaring developed in the Wasserkuppe mountains in Germany. The single seat training method was developed there in the 1920s in gliders such as the Stamer-Lippisch. Little by little, pupils flew higher and higher by themselves. This method worked for training pilots, but despite the frantic shouts of the instructors, there were many minor crashes. After World War II, two seat gliders were used instead, since the instructor could always take over the controls when the glider was in danger.

MODERN GLIDING

Today, many pilots fly their sailplanes and gliders just for pleasure. Other pilots fly in competitions, which are mainly about flying a route or distance as fast as possible.

The clue to finding good thermals is to look for **cumulus clouds**. To win a competition a pilot must find a good thermal, circle up and then fly fast while descending in a straight line to the next thermal. The pilot who finds the best thermals will come back to the airfield first and be the day's winner. Gliding is also about enjoying nature. Glider pilots often tell about fantastic flights circling in thermals with storks, buzzards, or other big birds.

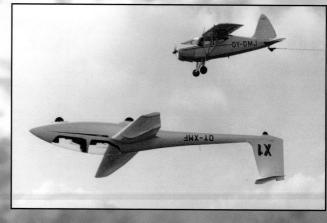

GLIDER AEROBATICS
Some gliders are good for aerobatics. This ASK-21 glider is flying upside down with the tow plane that pulled it up. The stunt was photographed for an aviation calendar.

DUO DISCUS
The Duo Discus is a tiny two seat glider that flies fast and smooth. Its design means it descends slowly and evenly.

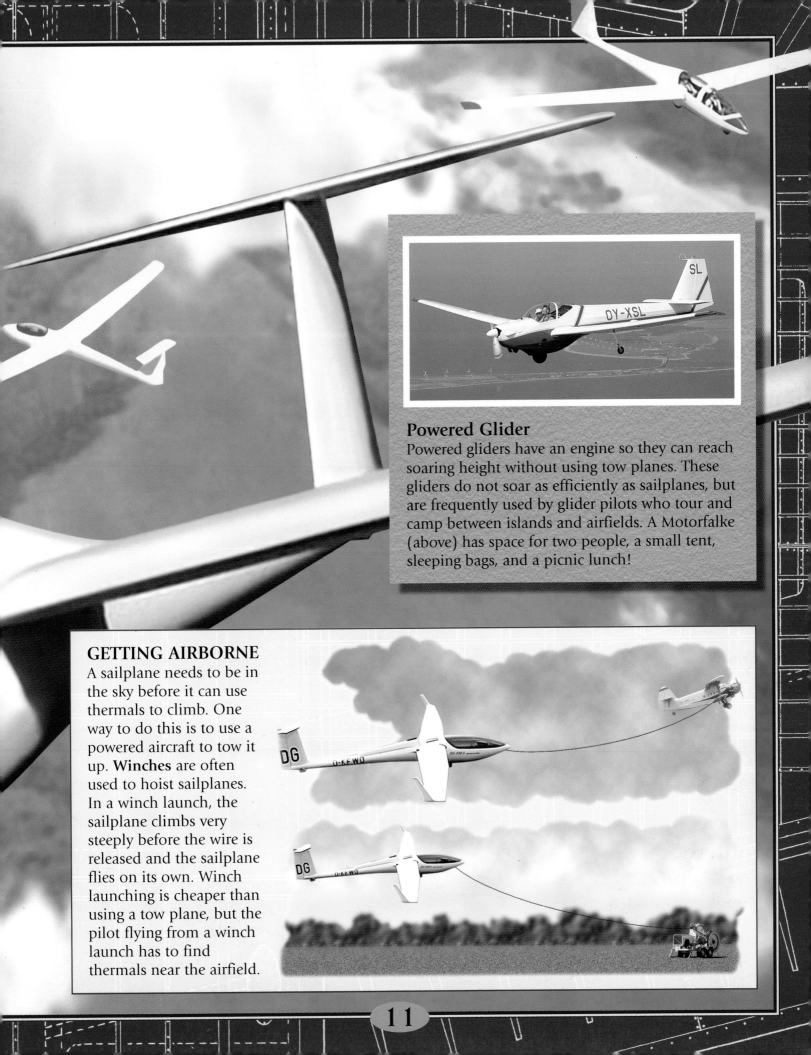

Powered Glider

Powered gliders have an engine so they can reach soaring height without using tow planes. These gliders do not soar as efficiently as sailplanes, but are frequently used by glider pilots who tour and camp between islands and airfields. A Motorfalke (above) has space for two people, a small tent, sleeping bags, and a picnic lunch!

GETTING AIRBORNE

A sailplane needs to be in the sky before it can use thermals to climb. One way to do this is to use a powered aircraft to tow it up. **Winches** are often used to hoist sailplanes. In a winch launch, the sailplane climbs very steeply before the wire is released and the sailplane flies on its own. Winch launching is cheaper than using a tow plane, but the pilot flying from a winch launch has to find thermals near the airfield.

CONTROL SURFACES

An aircraft is controlled by moving the ailerons and elevators with the control stick, or yoke in modern aircraft, while the **rudder** is moved with pedals. Normal handling of a plane is not difficult, but it takes a while to get used to using all three controls, to do even the simplest of maneuvers properly.

Rudder

Elevators

Ailerons

PIPER CUB

In the late 1930s, the Piper Cub was one of the most popular training aircraft. Today the two seat Cessna 150 is rarely used for this purpose. Most people learn to fly in slightly bigger aircraft, such as the Cessna 172 or Piper PA-28.

LEARNING TO FLY

Pilots never forget the moment the instructor steps out and tells them to fly a circuit of the airfield on their own. This is a pilot's first solo flight.

Before they ever fly solo, flying school students learn how to handle an aircraft: how to take off, fly straight, level, turn, and land. Student pilots must also try to stall the aircraft by reducing power and lifting the nose until the plane flies slower and slower. During a stall, small vibrations are a warning that the air no longer produces enough lift over the wings. When a plane stalls at a low altitude, a crash is likely. Flying school students train to avoid these stalls. Navigation, radio communications, and other skills are also taught at flight school. After logging 45 or 50 hours in the air flying, flight school students get their Private Pilot's License (PPL).

GIPSY MOTHS
In the late 1920s and 1930s, the de Havilland Gipsy Moth was very popular for flight training, touring, and even air racing. American pilot Laura Ingalls flew a record breaking 344 loops in her Gipsy Moth.

PA-28
The Piper PA-28 Archer is a popular four seat training and touring aircraft. Learning to fly with a nose wheel in today's aircraft is easier than handling a **tail dragger** such as the Piper Cub (left). Tail draggers are hardly ever used to train student pilots for their PPL, but some flying clubs keep them for specialized training.

DO-IT-YOURSELF

For some people, the ultimate challenge is building their own aircraft, sometimes even from their own design. Do-it-yourself, or homebuilt, aircraft are some of the most creative aircraft to fly.

FLYING FLEA

The Flying Flea was developed in the 1930s as an easy-to-build, easy-to-fly aircraft for new pilots. Unfortunately, some early versions of the Flying Flea crashed and it never became the success its designer had hoped it would be.

Most homebuilt aircraft are made from kits, such as the Europa and BD-5. Some homebuilts, such as the Hummel Bird and Jodel, are made from plans. To turn a kit into a finished aircraft takes years of work.

Homebuilders must be precise and accurate if they want their aircraft to be safe.

ULTIMATE
Country: Canada
Length: 17 ft 5 in (5.3 m)
Wingspan: 15 ft 10 in (4.8 m)
Speed: 150 mph (241 km/h)
First flown: 1986

One advantage of new homebuilt aircraft is that they often perform better than some factory built aircraft with the same size engines.

EUROPA
Country: Great Britain
Length: 19 ft 2 in (5.8 m)
Wingspan: 27 ft 2 in (8.3 m)
Speed: 152 mph (245 km/h)
First flown: 1992

JODEL
Country: France
Length: 20 ft 10 in (6.4 m)
Wingspan: 26 ft 10 in (8.2 m)
Speed: 80 mph (130 km/h)
First flown: 1950

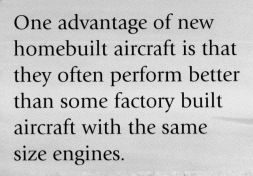

World Rounder

As a young boy, Jon Johanson did not do well in school. His early problems did not stop him from learning how to fly or build his own airplane. Johnson has flown his homebuilt aircraft around the world three times, from the east, the west, and over the top. Here he is a few days after flying across the North Pole in the aircraft he built himself.

BD-5
Country: USA
Length: 14 ft 8 in (4.5 m)
Wingspan: 21 ft 6 in (6.5 m)
Speed: 240 mph (386 km/h)
First flown: 1972

FALCO F.8

The Falco F.8 is a streamlined Italian aerobatic two seat glider built from wood. Today this aircraft is used for recreational flying. In the 1960s, it was equipped to air test instruments that were used in the development of the Concorde wing.

INSTRUMENTS AND CONTROLS – CESSNA 172

1. Airspeed indicator – how fast you are traveling through the air.
2. Artificial horizon – where the horizon is in relation to the aircraft, which is essential on cloudy days.
3. Altimeter – your height above sea level. 4. Vertical speed indicator – how fast you are climbing or descending. 5. Steering yoke.
6. Throttle. 7. Rudder pedals.

Modern light aircraft are well equipped with electronic equipment that make them easy and safe to fly. Most planes have two or four seats. They can take off from runways in big airports or from small strips of grass.

Many light aircraft in the air today are 20 or 30 years old. The late 1960s and '70s were the heyday of light aircraft production, when American companies built a total of 15,000 or more aircraft a year. The Cessna 172 and Piper PA-28 were among the most commonly produced aircraft. Many of these aircraft are still flying. Today most have **GPS** satellite navigation, which makes it easy for pilots to find their destination.

Touring

Imagine flying out to a small grass airfield with your friends or family, putting up a tent and sleeping under the wing. Light aircraft pilots do just this at "fly ins." Fly ins are parties where navigational competitions are held during the day and barbecues are held at night.

ULTRALIGHTS

Ultralights are personal flying crafts that are ideal for nature lovers. In Australia, people even take their ultralights out whale watching and kangaroo spotting.

HANG GLIDER
Today's hang gliders are simple aircraft, although they are made from modern, lightweight materials.

Hang gliders were the first personal flying crafts, although they were not called ultralights in the 1890s. The design of these early hang gliders was very simple. Today's ultralights are flown for fun and for adventure sports. Some are gliders that use only air power, while others are powered by motors. Trikes are powered hang gliders in which the pilot shifts body weight to turn the aircraft. A Weedhopper is controlled by a rudder and elevator like an airplane, but it does not have ailerons. Many radio-controlled model aircraft are controlled the same way.

PARAGLIDER
A paraglider is a steerable glider with inflatable wings. It can soar in thermals and cover long distances.

SCANDAL
The Scandal is a hang glider with a long wing that changes shape according to airspeed. It is more efficient at both high and low speeds than most other hang gliders.

The First Hang Glider
The world's first pilot, Otto Lilienthal, flew his hang gliders in the 1890s to learn to fly before moving to powered aircraft. He never built powered aircraft, as he was killed in a hang glider crash.

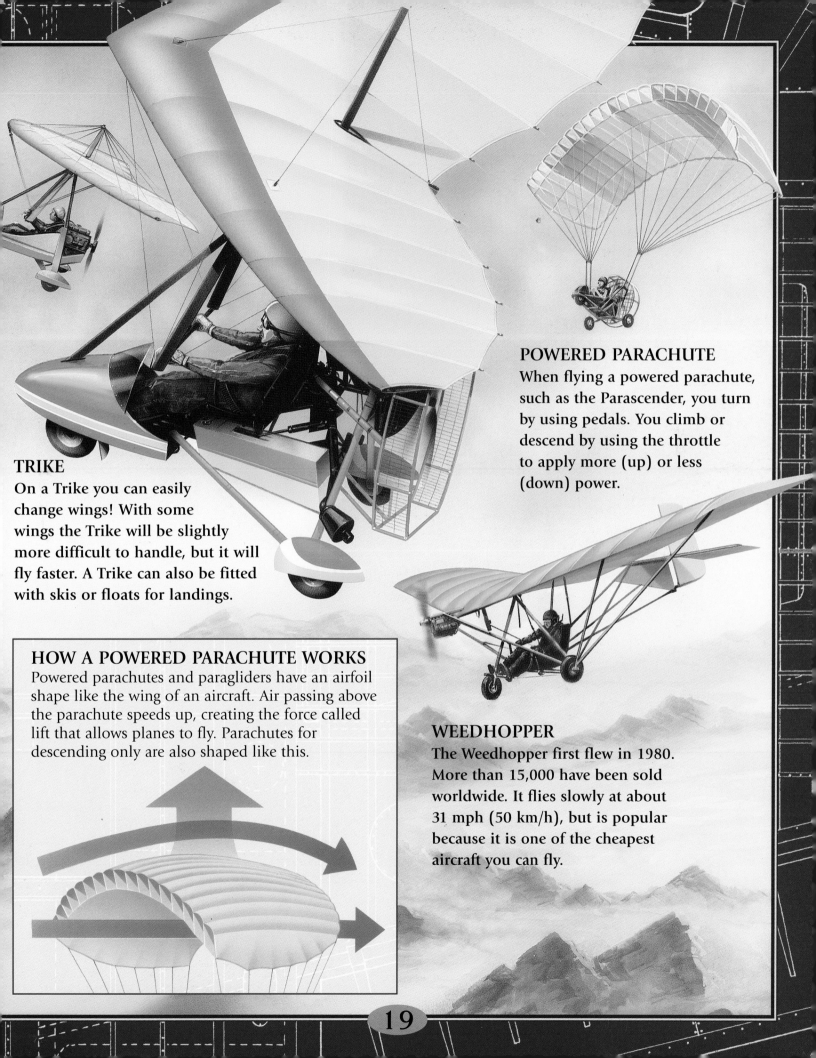

TRIKE

On a Trike you can easily change wings! With some wings the Trike will be slightly more difficult to handle, but it will fly faster. A Trike can also be fitted with skis or floats for landings.

POWERED PARACHUTE

When flying a powered parachute, such as the Parascender, you turn by using pedals. You climb or descend by using the throttle to apply more (up) or less (down) power.

HOW A POWERED PARACHUTE WORKS

Powered parachutes and paragliders have an airfoil shape like the wing of an aircraft. Air passing above the parachute speeds up, creating the force called lift that allows planes to fly. Parachutes for descending only are also shaped like this.

WEEDHOPPER

The Weedhopper first flew in 1980. More than 15,000 have been sold worldwide. It flies slowly at about 31 mph (50 km/h), but is popular because it is one of the cheapest aircraft you can fly.

AIR RACING

Pilots have been racing their aircraft against each other almost from the beginning of powered flight. Until World War II, racing aircraft were at the cutting-edge of aviation technology. Since the war, military jets have become the fastest aircraft. Air races are still flown today, and still attract large crowds.

THE FIRST AIR RACE

At the Gordon Bennett Trophy Race held at Reims, France in 1909, aircraft such as this Antoinette flew two 6.2 mile (10 km) laps as quickly as possible. American Glenn Curtiss won with his biplane, Reims Racer, flying at an average speed of 46.6 mph (75 km/h).

The National Championship Air Races that are flown each year at Reno, Nevada, are the most spectacular in the world. Aircraft compete in different classes and fly short courses at low level, so people on the ground have the best possible view of them. Between races, top aerobatic and show pilots entertain the crowds with stunts or formation flying. The unlimited class is mostly modified World War II fighters such as the Mustang, Bearcat, or Sea Fury. Record speeds of 497.787 mph (801.111 km/h) have been recorded at this event. Pilots must concentrate to fly their old planes low over the desert.

RENO RACING CLASSES

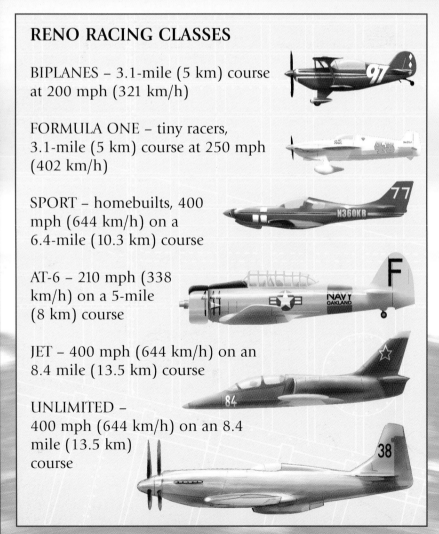

BIPLANES – 3.1-mile (5 km) course at 200 mph (321 km/h)

FORMULA ONE – tiny racers, 3.1-mile (5 km) course at 250 mph (402 km/h)

SPORT – homebuilts, 400 mph (644 km/h) on a 6.4-mile (10.3 km) course

AT-6 – 210 mph (338 km/h) on a 5-mile (8 km) course

JET – 400 mph (644 km/h) on an 8.4 mile (13.5 km) course

UNLIMITED – 400 mph (644 km/h) on an 8.4 mile (13.5 km) course

1930 NATIONAL AIR RACES
10TH ANNIVERSARY

THRILL FOR THE NATION!

CURTISS - REYNOLDS AIRPORT --- CHICAGO

Pre-war Circuit Racing

In the United States, aircraft raced at low level at the National Air Races during the 1930s. Speed rather than safety was the priority for aircraft designers. Some aircraft were dangerous to fly. One such aircraft was the Gee Bee racer, which was basically a huge engine with as small an airframe as possible behind it. In 1932, pilot Jimmy Doolittle won the Thompson Trophy by flying the Gee Bee racer at 296 mph (476 km/h), but he never wanted to fly it again. Other pilots took the risk and crashed doing so.

THE CHASE IS ON

At the races in Reno, aircraft fly on courses marked out by telephone poles with a striped drum at the top. The markers are 50 feet (15 m) tall and clearly visible for pilots to see when they are traveling at over 400 mph (644 km/h).

FLYING VINTAGE AIRCRAFT

When it comes to flying for fun, nothing beats a vintage aircraft. The open cockpit, the sound of wind in the wires, and the warmth of the sun all combine to make flying old planes unforgettable.

RESTORATION PROJECTS
It took this pilot and mechanic six years of his spare time to restore this 1940s Fairchild Argus.

Open cockpits are not as comfortable as the cabins of modern light aircraft, but flying in open cockpits on warm summer days is a lot of fun. Some vintage aircraft do have enclosed cabins, although they look very different from modern aircraft. Many people enjoy restoring their own vintage aircraft. Often they start with an old aircraft that looks like a total wreck. First, the wooden framework of the wings are carefully checked and often re-glued. The steel tube fuselage, or body, is inspected and the engine taken apart and overhauled, or repaired. The airframe is then covered in new fabric and painted. Restoring vintage aircraft is time consuming and expensive work.

Venerable Tiger Moth
During World War II, most of Britain's Royal Air Force pilots learned to fly in Tiger Moths. After the war many Tigers ended up at flying clubs, and are still flying today. Some people think a fabric covered biplane braced with struts and wires is fragile, but a Tiger Moth can do aerobatics that would pull the wings off many modern light aircraft!

TESTING THE FLYER

Replicas are new aircraft that are built to look like vintage aircraft. A replica of the Wright *Flyer*, the world's very first powered aircraft from 1903, is being tested by NASA. By flying and testing replicas, pilots can better understand the aircraft of the past.

BOEING STEARMAN

The Boeing Stearman is a powerful American World War II trainer. Stearmans are popular today with airshow pilots. The big engines easily pull the aircraft around in a loop, even with a wing walker adding extra drag to the aircraft.

AIRCRAFT GRAVEYARDS
The B-24 Liberators were destroyed after World War II. Many thousands of these warplanes were cut up when the war ended. Today, the few surviving warplanes are well looked after.

AP-004

The Beginner Warbird
Harvards were used as World War II trainers. They are still used as trainers today, more than 55 years later. Pilots who are used to modern aircraft fly the Harvards before progressing to the heavier, more demanding Mustangs, Spitfires, and other fighter planes. Harvards are also flown as warplanes.

WARBIRDS

It is interesting to see old aircraft in museums, but even more exciting seeing them fly. The high powered old warplanes are among the most popular performers at airshows.

Warplanes can be from World War I or the early jet age, but most warplanes flying today are World War II aircraft. They were the fastest **piston engined**, propeller driven aircraft built. They were expensive to build and operate, but effective in combat. Today, some warplanes are flown by museums or clubs, but many are owned and operated by companies that fly them at airshows or for movie work. Often, volunteers work restoring and keeping them in good condition because they want to keep them flying.

B-25 – FLYING MEMORIAL
Warplanes such as this B-25 Mitchell bomber are flown to commemorate those who fought and died in them.

STORMBIRDS – ME 262 PROJECT
The German twin jet Messerschmitt Me 262 "Stormbird" was one of the most advanced World War II fighter planes. A few still existed in museums, but none were flown as war planes. Then, a Me 262 was borrowed from a museum and taken apart for the parts to be copied. Five new ME 262s have now been built in the United States. The first one was test flown in 2002.

AEROBATICS

Aerobatics is a kind of flying where spectacular stunts are performed at high speeds. Often, the stunts are performed for crowds on the ground at airshows.

Aerobatic pilots control their aircraft while flying straight up, upside down, and in loops. There are hundreds of different aerobatic maneuvers, but all are made of four basic ones: the spin, roll, loop, and stall turn. During competitions and at airshows, pilots perform the maneuvers very precisely and within a small airspace. Often, they perform in tight formation with other planes. When flying, the pilots not only have to concentrate on their flying, but also compensate for drifting in the wind at the same time. When flying aerobatic displays at airshows, the aircraft sometimes use a smoke generator that leaves smoke trails in the sky.

FORMATIONS
Jet aerobatics flown in formation are done mostly by special military units, such as the U.S. Air Force Thunderbirds, who are famous for very tight F-16 formations. When in formation, each pilot looks at the other aircraft, keeping in position with them.

Yak-55
The Russian Yak-55 is a single seat aircraft designed for aerobatics. It weighs about the same as a four seat PA-28 light plane, but its 360 hp Yak engine is twice as powerful. The engine is needed to pull the Yak up in vertical climbs.

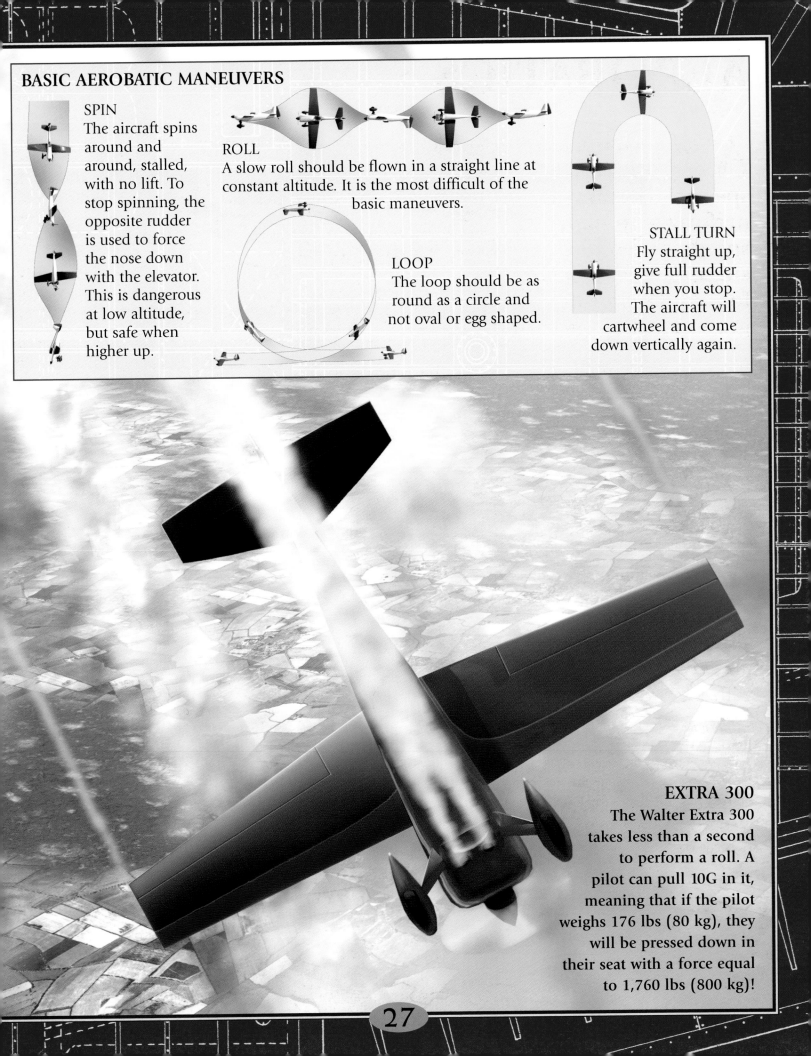

BASIC AEROBATIC MANEUVERS

SPIN
The aircraft spins around and around, stalled, with no lift. To stop spinning, the opposite rudder is used to force the nose down with the elevator. This is dangerous at low altitude, but safe when higher up.

ROLL
A slow roll should be flown in a straight line at constant altitude. It is the most difficult of the basic maneuvers.

LOOP
The loop should be as round as a circle and not oval or egg shaped.

STALL TURN
Fly straight up, give full rudder when you stop. The aircraft will cartwheel and come down vertically again.

EXTRA 300
The Walter Extra 300 takes less than a second to perform a roll. A pilot can pull 10G in it, meaning that if the pilot weighs 176 lbs (80 kg), they will be pressed down in their seat with a force equal to 1,760 lbs (800 kg)!

MODEL AIRCRAFT

Most model aircraft are radio controlled. Radio-controlled models are exactly like full size aircraft, apart from the fact that the pilots stand firmly on the ground and never suffer from air sickness.

There are models for all kinds of flying. Gliders are for thermal or slope soaring. Some slope soarers are built with fast jet shapes and look great when they streak past. Powered models can be built as trainers or for aerobatics. Scale models look just like real aircraft, down to tiny details, like rivet heads and exhaust stains.

Rubber Band Power

Today's rubber band powered contest models are high tech and built from carbon fiber, glass fiber, plastic covering, aluminum, and balsa wood. These "Wakefield" models climb up to 300 feet (91 m) and soar for a long time.

CONSTRUCTION TECHNIQUES

The "Berliner" has a wingspan of 87 inches (220 cm) and is built using traditional modeling techniques. The model has a balsa wood and plywood frame, with spruce and hardwood reinforcement. The model is covered in iron-on plastic film. Other models are built using fiberglass, carbon fiber, styrofoam, plastic, and even cardboard.

Berliner

Balsa frame

The "Berliner" (below left) was built for the simple purpose of giving teddy bears joy rides. Models can be built from kits, some of which require almost no building. Modelers often prefer to build from plans or design their own models. Modelers design aircraft at home, build it without spending a fortune, and then fly it from a field. Modelers are only limited by their own imagination.

R/C WHIRLYBIRDS
It takes a bit more patience and time to fly radio controlled helicopters.

FLY YOUR OWN FIGHTER
With radio-controlled models you can fly your own fighter plane like this Messerschmitt Bf 109. Experienced modelers make the landing gear retractable, as on the real aircraft.

SPOTTERS' GUIDE

These aircraft illustrate the wide variety people use for touring, competitions, racing, or just for fun. An aircraft such as the Piper Cub is common, simple, and easy to fly. The Racing Sea Fury is best described as a hot rod that you need a lot of experience to master. The glider is the cheapest way to fly.

CASSUTT
Country: USA
Description: Single seat racer
Length: 16 ft (4.9 m)
Wingspan: 15 ft (4.6 m)
Speed: 230 mph (370 km/h)

PIPER CUB
Country: USA
Description: Light training and touring aircraft
Length: 22 ft 4 in (6.8 m)
Wingspan: 35 ft 2 in (10.7 m)
Speed: 85 mph (137 km/h)

RACING SEA FURY
Country: Great Britain
Description: Fighter modified for racing
Length: 34 ft 8 in (10.6 m)
Wingspan: 38 ft 5 in (11.7 m)
Speed: 527 mph (850 km/h)

BOEING STEARMAN
Country: USA
Description: Vintage aircraft
Length: 24 ft 9 in (7.5 m)
Wingspan: 32 ft 2 in (9.8 m)
Speed: 140 mph (225 km/h)

YAK-52
Country: Russia
Description: Aerobatic trainer
Length: 25 ft 5 in (7.8 m)
Wingspan: 30 ft 6 in (9.3 m)
Speed: 186 mph (300 km/h)

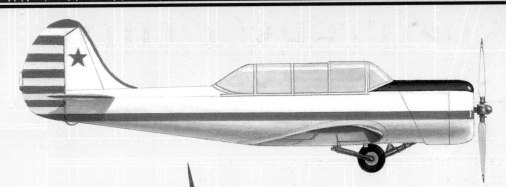

WALTER EXTRA 300
Country: Germany
Description: Aerobatic aircraft
Length: 23 ft (7 m)
Wingspan: 25 ft 3 in (7.7 m)
Speed: 213 mph (343 km/h)

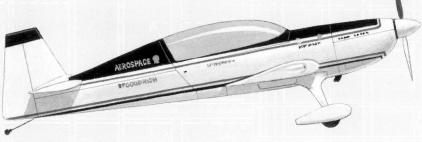

PITTS SPECIAL
Country: USA
Description: Aerobatic aircraft
Length: 17 ft 9 in (5.4 m)
Wingspan: 20 ft (6 m)
Speed: 152 mph (245 km/h)

DISCUS
Country: Germany
Description: Competition glider
Length: 22 ft 2 in (6.8 m)
Wingspan: 48 ft 9 in (14.8 m)
Minimum sink rate:1 ft 11 in (0.6 m) per second

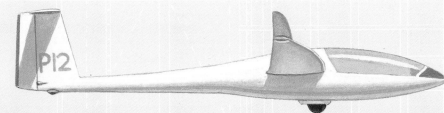

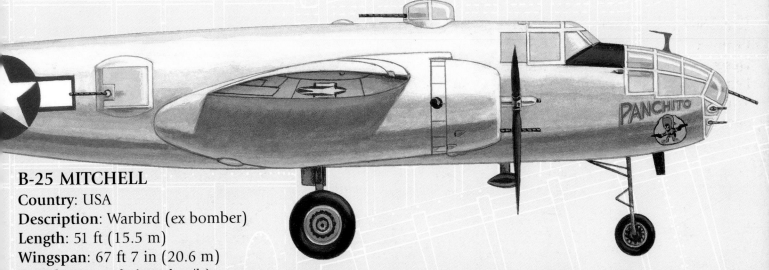

B-25 MITCHELL
Country: USA
Description: Warbird (ex bomber)
Length: 51 ft (15.5 m)
Wingspan: 67 ft 7 in (20.6 m)
Speed: 275 mph (443 km/h)

INDEX

GLOSSARY

AEROBATICS Stunts performed in an aircraft.

AIRSHIP A self-propelled aircraft filled with a lighter than air gas.

ALTITUDE A height measured from sea level or the Earth's surface.

ASCENT Rising upward.

BIPLANE An airplane with two sets of wings, one above the other.

CUMULUS CLOUDS Dense, white clouds that form when air cools and condenses as it rises. The rising air helps gliders lift from the ground.

DESCEND To come down.

DRAG The pulling force against the aircraft.

FLAMMABLE A material that ignites and burns easily.

GPS Global Positioning System, a worldwide navigational system that uses 24 satellites positioned around the world to calculate an object's position, or location on Earth.

HOMEBUILT Aircraft built at home, from a modeler's own plan or a modeling kit.

PISTON ENGINE A circular disk that moves back and forth in a cylinder. In engines, pistons are moved by igniting fuel and air.

RUDDER A hinged piece on the tail that is used to help steer the aircraft.

STALL TURN An aerobatic maneuver in an aircraft.

TAIL DRAGGER A type of powered aircraft that has a tailwheel instead of a nosewheel. It drags its tail across the ground during takeoff and landing.

TOW PLANE A powered plane that tows gliders into the air.

VINTAGE An old or antique aircraft.

WINCHES A motor driven or hand powered lifting machine with a rope that attaches to the load to be lifted.

WORLD WAR I An international war war fought from 1914 to 1918.

WORLD WAR II A war fought from 1939 to 1945 in which Great Britain, France, the Soviet Union, the United States, and other Allies defeated Germany, Italy, and Japan.